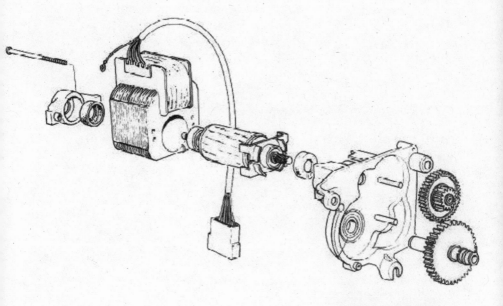

drive

Chris Pannell
drive

Cover and author photographs: Janice Jackson
Cover design: Leigh Kotsilidis
Typeset in: Eurostile
Printed by Coach House Books
Toronto, Canada

    Canadian   Patrimoine
Heritage   canadien

The publisher gratefully acknowledges the
support of the Canada Council for the Arts,
the Ontario Arts Council and the Book Publishing
Industry Development Program (BPIDP) for their
financial assistance.

Wolsak and Wynn Publishers Ltd
#102–69 Hughson Street North
Hamilton, ON
Canada L8R 1G5

Library and Archives Canada Cataloguing in Publication

Pannell, Chris, 1956–
        Drive / Chris Pannell.

Poems.
ISBN 978-1-894987-33-2

        I. Title.
PS8581.A64D75 2009   C811'.54   C2009-900052-0

Contents

Alternative Destinations

Behind the Wheel

Dream Bus

I am driving a school bus through
an Alex Colville painting.
The moon is setting after a full night
of wrecking sleep.
Creamy and large at the horizon
bitter to the tongue, she makes me ashamed
of my weak headlights
lies I told today.

She sprinkles salt on
the trees and road, turns them blue
too indigo to bear —
now she's down to the rim
of the sky, oval and orange —
fields of snow rise and
take her full belly into their valleys and creeks.
Tomorrow night
hundreds of premonitions
will rise, stone white
to be bathed by brushes.

In the corner of my eye
the painter's pallet flashes
and I floor it
all thirty-eight feet of straight lines and red lights
rip into the curve
Steel screams against the guard rail
cables and wooden posts pop free
staples from the tight canvas
fly past the windshield and
the collapsing frame
straight
into the gully
of pine
darkness.

One Dark Morning

Through rows of silent school buses
         I go
with bobbing flashlight, cold keys in hand
      for the one I will cajole to start.
Underfoot: frozen mud
a parking lot   icy ruts in which to twist
         an ankle

Stop. Look up. Click off my beam.
The stars say I'm innocent, flimsy as a flashlight.
Only morning air can bring out such clear
fears —
trapped where I don't belong
        here
     with an airport runway over the fence
a Great Escape seems possible
through any frozen field
       a Fokker triplane comes
       straight down
       one roaring engine, propeller, machine gun
       while I leap to catch the axle of its landing gear.

The moon makes brilliant the dirt and frost
makes the world as deep as calligraphy
divine signs in windows —
Holy Name of Mary
St. Bernadette and *Blessed Spirit.*

Still. I am early
and moving again along a row of bus grilles

The mechanical world is Off.
Do Not Pass While Signals Flashing.
Do Not Pass. Do Not Pass.
Watch Your Step.

Yellow, yellow, aurora glow
red tail lights will start to show
clearance, overheads, flashers, brake.
As I inspect the seventy-eight things I must inspect
night recedes into diesel fumes —
other drivers will soon be here for their assigned machines
they will follow me through the gate
for a street or two in the shimmying dark
then like deaf optimists, we will all shout and grin
and wave as we peel away
heading off
into sunlight.

Stopping the Bus by Woods on a Snowy Evening

The heaters have run long
and fashioned us into a snug little oven.
After a hard day at school
my last two teenagers doze
heads aslant on each other, near the back.
They are recharging themselves
before they face parents
or some other form of responsibility.
Their soft faces and closed eyes
warm me, and I look left
at snow, frozen pond
tire on a swing.

We wait for traffic
on Highway Five, see
a huge oak bough fallen
bark glistening with ice —
all is still but for the crackling radio.

Intersection clear: I should take them home.

Tonight fir trees draped in frost
was all it took to slow my driving to a crawl
until I thought I might throw open
the doors of my schedule and
run into those woods: *lovely, dark and deep*

The girl speaks, the boy replies
and I anticipate their stops
accelerate into night
remembering how
thirty-six empty seats will
follow me all the way to sleep.

Distant Lovers

It was a time of secrecy.

On the two-way radios that every driver
could hear
she spoke of
dispatching and destinations
added codes and hints, sighs and jokes.
Silently she cried of the deceit
for her unsaid words of love.

Every day, as he swung his bus
through its route
he listened for the special way she said
his name, imagined her dresses, her hands on her hips.
He could guess what she was about to say.
Each thrilled to the sound
of the other one's voice —
such likely and logical statements
they made to the air.

One of them should have died at this point
and given the story a tragic twist
but instead they bought wireless email devices
and began to tap out invitations
to rendezvous after work —
these appointments often had to be broken
for a propaganda event or chores with a significant other
someone always needed
to be consoled.

And when they began to lose their clever voices
listeners who might have guessed
what was in play
were left to imagine kisses
to imagine other fingers unbuttoning other clothes

as if what happened had become a film
we watched
       in a cool theatre on a hot day
about lovers living through a war.

Blue over Rockton

I drive the homebound
school bus
with all the time I need among these farms
for revving and slowing, for looking at the cold
autumn afternoon, imagining snow.
      A grey cat in a mown field
           watches me approach and I think
      Don't Run Under My Wheels.

        Five six zero running eight minutes late
      I say to the dispatcher, the fleet
is elsewhere, with its own problems.

Three months into this job, and I am
years late, years behind
      I know not what.
My frequent dreams of squandered time
are withering into a truth, like the image
in the overhead mirror of my last passenger —
a teenage boy looking out the window
at the bright maple trees —
      And behind the farmhouse, a rusting yellow bus
      is missing some windows and doors.

If I could escape, I'd take my
eyes off the road, risk the
culvert, take that curve on faith.
At sixty kilometers per hour I'd get out my notebook and write —
      bright pumpkins button a field
      of woven rust — a tweed jacket, while
      cabbages ripple green, purple out an ocean
      my creaky engine at full throttle through the gullies
      every hill, a swelling wave.

A combine cut
that exhausted corn yesterday

and gathered up its long-grassed sensibility
its broad-leaf sentiments, leaving ruts and stems
rows of stubble. They look like sewn seams
holding down the black earth
holding down my belief in *next year*
that the kernels within the cobs are
bullets of hard hope —
        whispers of sustenance
        sleepy mumbles
        from those silos by the red barn.

I Have Thirty Minutes

        to write a poem on city time
between these lights changing
during this wave of
bicycles, pedestrians, and pick-up trucks
        to observe the world beyond
this windshield, at the intersection of
ambition and interruption.

In my bus I carry the human cargo —
post-brain injury, post-heart attack, post-hip replacement.
A cynic among the lambs asks me
Wheelchairs, canes, bundles of steel, what's the difference?

He thinks his fellow passengers
are a logistical
problem to be solved
that he and his scooter are two
different kinds of cargo.
Perhaps he has devalued the whole business of living
or taken my bus for a moving van.

All I can say is, *We'll talk later* —
which is what I said to my wife this morning
when she asked when we were going to write our wills
and me in a rush to start my shift.

On my lunch half-hour
I remember my last will and testament
and wonder what kind of duty or deadline
it would take for me
to separate myself
from the world of things.

The Way She Loves Him

On the bus
he glares
        as if angry to be out of the hospital
then all feeling seems to swing
with his eyes, away to the starlings we can hear outside the window
as dark as questions in the trees.

He's been dressed in a ball cap
grey sweats, and a red plaid coat.
The chrome wheelchair
like a throne, empowers him
with equipment behind:
feeding bag on a hook, tube to stomach
a square solid-state ventilator, an oxygen tank.
I strap his chair to the floor
ratchets click, struts creak —
I slide a seatbelt under his limp, warm arms.

For every grunt
        a response from her:
What a great Sunday this will be
This bus will take us straight home
Your brother Henry's coming over   *a barbeque like before.*

We pull away and soon we pass a field
stubbled with shafts of last year's corn
the next field has been neatly ploughed.
Perhaps he knows farming from the inside out
or has an opinion on how all these acres of earth became
acres of housing for the people who live on
Grassyplain Drive or Hawkswood Trail.

His mouth, dry and ajar, is hard to close.
Her lips quiver and she resumes her conversation
with the man he was, hovers
like a bee above a flower, yet
he cannot turn to look at her.

Half-way down the escarpment, crows perch on the rock-strewn
sides that crumble, like memories.
I imagine he's searching
for a place under trees, for a spot of brown
that will take him, so he might escape
everything in her voice
it does no good to hear.

Poem for the Houses on Ann Street

Every day
the children of Ann Street board my bus
while the minute hand of my watch
sweeps from seven to eight. They swish by me
in the driver's seat. Most flutter to the back —
a snowy owl, sparrows, chickadees —
a few older ones come as deer, coyotes, and
one is a bear cub who sits in the first seat behind me
staring down my neck, licking his canines and
exhaling hot breath.

Their parents expect me at 8:36
and not believing in metamorphosis they weigh
their children down with little suitcases, knapsacks and
wireless technology —

But no one can discipline the wilderness.
The last one boarded, I close the doors
and I'm contained, penned in by chattering
child-life.

We turn from Ann Street and I am Noah —
obliged to keep a giggling, screeching
ark on course. In the school parking lot
a few teachers will be waiting —
when we come into port, they will wave
like dock-hands, tether us back to the earth.
The bus will rock gently as the creatures disembark.

My Car

One winter morning, I found my car warm
and bare of snow. It had been racing overnight —
trying to overcome some fears —
of sliding from the road, tires plugged with mud
of rolling over and over in the hay, alone.

I'm afraid we have watched
too many movies at the drive-in together.
Too many street-racing scenes.
Too many romances in foreign countries
where the car
was the star.

Now it slouches between concrete pillars in public
garages, dreams of being discovered by
a Hollywood director — seems disappointed
when approaching footfalls
are mine.

It hates the mechanic and hides any illness
I report. The transmission shifts silently for him
grinds noisily in my hand.
The plug has fused to the oil pan rather than release
its blackened blood. The fuel gauge bounces up and down
like a grasshopper in the breeze.
The radio drifts off signal, or goes dead.

Only the steering wheel still loves me — for my fingers' firmness
across its curve, for my massaging palms, drumming thumbs
while we wait at an intersection.

The driver-side window creaks and sticks when
I draw near the police spot-check at Christmas.
Perhaps my car is trying
like a child who knows the parental flaw
to protect me as best it can.

50 Charlton Avenue East

At St. Joseph's Hospital a thousand lights shine
in the pharmacy, operating rooms, and halls
while massive air conditioners on the roof
roar like my bus mechanic's pneumatic tools.
At the edge of town, the transit garage works all night
getting buses ready for the morning.
Imagine one up on a hoist
a lamp on a wire in the space beneath
flickering as the mechanic moves
with his shadow.

Melvin Greenberg grins to see me, his scheduled ride home.
        I don't know much about dialysis,
                but my friend refused it, Melvin says, *and died.*
I wonder if he couldn't stand
the trip every other day, couldn't stand
to enter the electric hum of the unknown
the inexplicable way his body
had become toxic to him.

Melvin and I natter like brothers
we are devices that can be friends.
His surgeon and my bus mechanic
have much in common
but unlike motors our hearts
frighten easily, we are ready to mourn
when the paperboy arrives
to see ourselves in the obituaries
lover of Annabel, grandfather of Marilyn
business partner of Benjamin and Saul.

The hospital does not think
any more than Melvin's Lincoln
sitting in his driveway for six months
misses him. It is no horse
there are no forests near Forest Ave.
from which we might be born again.

The hospital can make us live
but only until the day we each return
preceded by shadows
for one final, systemic halt.

On a Warm Day, Gavin MacKinnon

grunts and calls through the window
to the girl in the white summer frock
whose hair is long and blonde
who is so delicious
that most men would be speechless
admiring
her steady gait, her eternal pride.

Gavin cannot restrain himself
despite wheelchair, lap table, seatbelt —
he starts to thrash and
wave his arms, his mouth twists and
        oooohhhhh
and again Oh?
and Heyyyyyyy!!

He is channelling his heartbeat
along with all the heat and humidity
of an August day —
his fine soft hair
falls in his eyes and he beams
because he knows about the lift of her ass
as she walks, though he has never stood erect.
He waves and rolls his head
and his feet thrash, and one comes down
        between
his chair's footrests, finds the floor
pounds hard upon the grey
non-slip surface, pounds and pounds
and sneaker-prints his mark.
He throws himself side to side
against the floor attachments —
the bolts in his wheelchair groan and clank
as they loosen. Gavin can make
      the world
tilt off its axles.

We pull away from the red light, he twists his head to her —
his fingers grabbing the window frame.

She has not seen or heard him, but I have to agree
with everything he has said
about her beauty.

Taking a DARTS Bus Through Hess Village

Hess Village wishes it was Westdale or Ancaster
where on a few of the older cul-de-sacs
real money lives, with gardeners.
Hess Street: university students
bars, real estate investments
physio clinics, dentists and profit statements.

The diners on the patios
can hardly be happy to see me and Sam
in a DARTS bus, crawl down the cobblestone lane
behind a Mercedes, a Ford Expedition
and a halting Chevy.

Sam is elderly, he trembles and
mucus dangles from his nose
as he stares out
his wide window, waves his aluminum cane
with its rubber foot at pedestrians
at the diners on the patio.
Imported beer and Sunday lunches
possibly go down
a little less easy after
the sight of Sam's gappy gums
his distended rotten teeth.

If he could rise out of his wheelchair
what would they think of his grey cardigan
its gravy stains and open pockets
like nests, emptied of birds?
Hearing aids protrude —
wires down the back of his neck
remind me of wires that keep us going
hidden behind the dashboard
that slowing feeling when I touch the brakes.

In the Woods at Ancaster High

Acorns fall like bullets through the boughs
and beetles cling to the undersides
            of swaying leaves
There's no room to seed another tree
this hail of wood will
rot upon the forest floor —

Spiderwebs bind the tops of weeds
make a trap where bugs will gather
and never leave.
A chipmunk springs and his tail
brushes a web, and part of someone's domain is gone.
She appears within a minute
and begins the repair —
flies and mosquitoes being
what she needs, and a male of her own kind
not unlike the girls out of school
who ride bikes on Jerseyville Road —

A trio of butterflies: erratic in air
dispense charm like pollen
their colour cast off in the lazy manner
of the slouch, the amble
unaware their hues and wingspan
are for a reason
like themselves, out so early
on a cool summer morning.

Every Few Days

I take the same group of passengers to dialysis —
from their walkers and scooters they glare at a pedestrian
who can sprint through the traffic on Charlton on legs
who is oblivious to a wheelchair
rolling down this ramp into the great outdoors.

Every few days someone in our group
has lost a toe or part of a leg to surgery
bits of themselves gone, along the route to home
or hospital.

Every few days I have to tell myself
not to muddle up my point of view with theirs.
I am not a tumbrel driver
though my uniform is black. The passengers envy me
that I can die at home in bed
rather than fall apart in public.

We takes and we delivers
we are the gear-men and women, with our hands on the wheel
who can always find the front porch light
glimmering in the dark, the signal of a worried wife.

We are staring at our own death
strapping ourselves in for our own safety —
a redundant foot rest on a wheelchair
a bandaged stump within an inch of my face
his tears I learn to see
but I keep my eyes on the cup of ice in his hands
cold water all he can take after four hours
of cleansing his own blood every few days
by machine.

The Man Who Never Had a Chance

He's not an easy passenger —
all wheelchair and splinted right hand.
He Shouts.   Each.   Word.
Is quick to anger, demands a cigarette from me.

The other drivers say he was born to alcoholics
who dropped him on his head
                    when he was a baby.

It's noon and it's hot
and the air conditioning on this bus
                              barely works.

We are both stiffening
                    cranky
hunched over   different kinds of wheels.

I show him less kindness   than I should.
It takes effort to   . stop pitying myself
soaked in sweat
to remember   we live
                         in vastly different
                    illusions.

He shouts *Radio!*
so I make it rock
loud enough that we might both forget ourselves —

But when we arrive
at Chedoke Hospital, I turn it down again
and watch
two tiny paraplegic girls learning to
drive their power wheelchairs along summer walkways —
chairs as small as toys they'll soon
outgrow. Their instructor walks ahead
looks back, shouts when one gets stuck
nothing less than complete self-reliance will do
in a two-legged, step-up-against-gravity kind of world.

My fifty-year old passenger gurgles
then shouts
Radio!   Up!
as if to say
Hey Driver, get over it.
Go get the one we came for
then take me to the pool.

A bus may be musical

because
in the driver's ear
wind at the windows is shaped
by forward movement —
compressors and fan belts take parts
in an urgent orchestra —
mechanisms cry melody
and because the driver is keen
to conduct and please himself —
the four wheels thrum
and bounce a bass
from the earth itself

The Test

The driver sweeps the bus and among
the hair elastics, dead batteries, and juice boxes
he finds *Pretest: Reproductive Physiology*
Match the following terms with the statements below them.

Tape hangs from the back of a seat, a six inch
tear in the upholstery. *Melissa is a whore.*
Rock against Racism. Fuck you.
This bus smells like puke.

He can't find the answer from the choices offered.
A vast group of microscopic tubes where sperm are stored.
He tucks away the broom and thinks of those who greet
him as they get on. He will always care more
for them than they for him. He is overwhelmed with
responsibility.
He watches two girls sprint
across the parking lot as the bell rings.
He wishes he was a teacher.

Steam rises from the candy factory across the street. If it's January
they will be making Valentine sweets. In February, they will
make Easter chocolate. Though he was late to every stop this morning
the boy with blond dreadlocks was later
and rushed across a busy road as he turned the bus into a side street.

One should never argue with a teenager.
The correct answer is to stop driving for a high school.

The School Bus Driver Says Goodbye to All That

Poetry is the granny of literature
in the corner, minding her
knit one, purl two.
We only call on the old girl in times
of catastrophe such as war
or
when we fall in love —
she barely listens to what we say.

Today we are asking for a poem that says:
Goodbye bus shelters with
your witty advertising written upscale of us.
Goodbye, new tractor on top of a building.
Goodbye billboard model
in a swimsuit running a treadmill in your home
exercising your right to arouse me
from behind the North 52 Service Centre.

Goodbye Rockton, nestled in the frozen dark.
Every morning I've waited here to pick up the fruit of your loins
for his education in the city. Bye little bedroom lights
and yellow kitchens that mark the way for itinerant travellers.
My toes were always cold.

Goodbye Dundas, complex warren
of social climbers, your gorgeous kids full
of trouble and obedience and contradictions.

Goodbye to all that.

In the Air

At Wanuskewin, Saskatchewan

Prairie marmots have hundreds
of tunnels under this dry grass, to be safe
from hawks and the big blue air.
When I tipped my hat to the valley
to the hard work of the gentle creek
it blew away; now I hang on the edge
of a picnic table, at the brim of the plain.

The wind moans demolition orders
against this wooden lean-to.
In the museum
a medicine man
shakes his spear
dances his ancient dream.
Thousands of beads sing on his warrior
chest and ankles. *Spirits, help us*
find the buffalo herd
keep it in range of our hunger.

Outside, in the cooling dusk
I remember what he was too polite to say:
how Europeans ran like rats
onto the American prairie
slaughtered buffalo
from moving trains, poisoned the air
with oil wells.

The marmots have adjusted their snouts
toward the dumpster, air presses the flavour
of hamburger grease into their whiskers
the magpie can smell it too.
I want to see stars through teepee walls of soft

tanned bison hide, take the shelter of an ancient nation.
Styro cups and plates against the fence.
How I envy the magpie her escape
the wind-sloped trees in which she has built her nest.

Impression from a High Place

Night draws its raven black
negligee round the head of the city;
he can see his own nostalgia for
Fredericks of Hollywood, for what is
ancient, exciting black and whites
girlie-mags that were so out there
as hot as the smell of pot
summer sweat, nights on a porch.

Another twelve hour trip to commuterville
has extinguished the sensational inner life
of every driver. No one had time to admire
the half-moon against that indigo drape.
Clouds like flour and dough
slide over the windshield
behind glasses and under eyelids
as regret.

Close to home, and around the corner
high heels halt, streetwalkers in tight jeans yawn
lights wink out.
On the escarpment, all is calm.

In the bay
under choppy, ghostly water
floats the body
of the past.

Swallows

swing out
flit back
across the Grand River
to a row of nests cemented
with excrement
to a steel girder
under the Footbridge Road bridge

the blue sky like a cup
brimming over
with fat white clouds

the swallows swoop and glide
catch mosquitoes that rise
from still water beyond the rock
where mosquitoes can breed in peace
before feeding themselves to the flock

from the shore I watch
their quickness of feather
I'll suffer these ankle bites to linger
with their dedication to movement
to random snaps of wing
to aeronautics and guidance to targets
only they can see, then
as a wave feels the moon
each swallow finds her own pulsing chicks
hunger incarnate
open mouths, sacs of skin

these parental black marks of hope
zip into the shade
then back   back
like pure desire
into the warming light

Sketch

When a bird prepares to die
he takes a lifetime's load
off the feet on which
he has fed and fought
bred and slept.

For the first time ever
he rests the knuckles and tendons
from which he has taken off
and the toes on which he has landed
over twelve years. There will be no
response to the chattering flock of the morning.

The body will be found with eyes
partly closed, wings
drawn snug as a cape.
There may be a few green feathers out of place
on the chest where he rests on his keel bone
this first and final time.

And his toes
now curl gently, feet side by side
once pink, now blue-veined
and greying by the hour
they softly stiffen in the rest
that only death provides
claws pinch sharply
at the nothing of the day.

Heart

feet, under the table
above, folded hands
in the middle space, the heart
                    yearns
            as it has for many years
to be filled, to live in some other house —
            air moves gently
                            at the window

the heart makes a fool of the machine
            mere pump and wheel
                    clank and squeak —
it responds to a higher chord
            and will follow melody into
                    the long darkness ahead

                some hearts find it easy
            to catch a breeze and rise into the night
others stay seated
                    their terrible loneliness
a weight in four chambers
each room
            a kind of desire

do not shout about
            what is obvious —
a heart is not an ear
            neither can it smile
                    it can only spread its wings
                    when it feels the wind approach

tell me

who can live entirely in love?
or give their love away like an adopted child?

why did mrs. stewart, our devout neighbour
stop her praying one spring day
to peer out
through her sheers
as my friends and the tennis ball of playoff hockey
bounced wild on the drive?

tell me now my love
if that slapshot went in the
tattered goal and out
the other side

love talk

for janice

1.

                    u start with
the twenny-furst letter in the alpha
bet u think eyem solip
                              sistic
looping werds around
              till all their
meanyness is gone
                  mere perfume lingering
                  like a nose over brandy
in a glass

i sing free of friction
sling my self into other guises
disguises to tell a story
bpNichol banished the)*%()*@.!
punctuation mark

                        damn right
without capitalizing on his
dropping caps from Everything
eyed like to draw your attention to what
comes naturally   a play
ing with words   the play's the thing
thing king too much about talk
is like trying to use your brain to breathe
which we do aujomagically
or not at all

2.

love is my lingua engla, my angielsku
a language on any other tongue would
taste as sweet

translated into common
clusters
            would talk many
more ways
            across borders
                        under blankets

let us be new notions under no god
caress each other with an honest
cry
lets be one body that mutters
            and talks to itself
using only synonyms for heart
relieve me-with-u
            u-with-me

a palindrome
            or pleasure dome of love

They Made Love

Tickle touch an inside joke
time becomes a text
they've already lived
anniversaries, shared disasters and care

two characters and a problem
call it love
their two lives make a novel
but
press down on the right word, right button
and a poem opens
like a violin case
lines as levers

stanza break, a cup of space
spills over the fluid lip of love

he's a shout
a vowel in a field
        give up your flower my love
        your Venus power
        has drawn me in, now lay down

she won't plant any more commas
in their garden
it's gonna storm
words
starting with   rain

A Song for Aging

Ears know when your key turns the lock
how your foot falls. After middle age, they begin to ring
like a minor sixth chord
too much exposure to melodrama
and electric guitars.

Lips, exhausted and thin
keep turning things down
are afraid of having
to clean up afterwards.

Eyes want to propose to the twenty-year-old
who's moved in next door
claim to know foreign languages
and exotic lands, are oblivious
to the bald dome above them. Hands wave
and sigh, sing snatches of the old songs
slap thighs with laughter.

Ears remember that convention
in Regina, ask my Throat if I'm still smoking.
Right Foot tells the story, and gets the details wrong
about how we walked a dog named Flea into a field
near your parents' house
and laid down our love with
grasshoppers on my back
and the sunlight in your eyes.

Tonight, Before Your House

Bathed in white and
        gold Christmas lights
the snow is crisp
        my hands are cold —
this house, no longer in your family
you, no longer in your family
you went —
        like an earthquake
through a hospital room

I miss
your voice
tonight, your friendly grey eyes
so clear
about the future
It's gone: especially
the future
                from which you leaned back
turned your face

Against this velvet blue night, the houses
on Abbey Close are lit up
for the baby Jesus and Santa Claus
I remember a few
        summer beers in your backyard
and trivial things, a glass you broke by accident —
and who would make it first to retirement?

I lean against the side of my car
my feelings in the trunk like a hostage
I cannot dispose of you —
your giant spruce towers above the roof
and points toward a highway
a double yellow line in the sky.

Night slides

        into the city
as soft as the veil his mother would adjust
around her bouffant hair before church

he drives his huge bus gently
up a cut in the escarpment's side
his good hand on the wheel
the other cradled in his lap —
he wears a shirt of blues
savours the squeaks and echoes
of the empty bus
and nothing but inky indigo ahead —
pink clouds in the west, above the lake —
from Concession Street the city
begins to perforate
with electric light

then he remembers: he is responsible —
tonight at those stops, everyone waited patiently
to descend into those lights
to connect with some love, some purpose
before a fault, either in the city's power grid
or in themselves
winks them out

near midnight, he tells his dispatcher
that he's clear (of passengers, of obligation)
he means he's clear of everything,
except a city spread beneath his eye
like an enormous tray of diamonds.

Taking Off from Regina

Wind ripples the short grass
by the runway
God's brush grooming the land
a force that carries rivulets and tides
and prairie birds into patterns of departure

Our silver plane
slowly increases engine speed
to a clumsy acceptable roar and after
driving around the concrete plain a while
we shudder into air, set our minds north
The clouds beneath swell
infinitely bright and blinding
not supporting even the idea
of a foot or finger —

To leave this plane with its movie
food and litter, I would need wings of
miraculous blue and
a bird's eye-brain coordination
I would leap off those riveted steel things
outside my window
and be drawn into the glistening air

like extended soft skin
longing to couple with the sky

Long Distance

London, After the Landmarks

After the clanging bells
of St. Paul's and the jack-hammering on Cannon Street
and the huff puff crowd
mobile phone yakking
steadily hopping curbs and jumping queues
flowing down cobbled lanes and staircases
to tube trains, oblivious to anthrax headlines
at news agents
stopping somewhere out of the wind
to light a fag.

The traffic rumble at a distance envelops
Hyde Park, like a mechanical bass
note on the earth's organ,
and yet it does not threaten me
near the bird sanctuary. There I perch
on a bench after an indigestible
Happy Meal from McDruids
employer of choice for sullen
teens, where the death of a young person's hope
is most profoundly realized
like a packet of ketchup
pierced and splattered under a shoe.

Who knows how feels this girl from
Poland who struggles with my food order
her lexicon shrunken to the scope
of a menu. By mid-afternoon, light is waning
the power walkers are coming through
they slide ahead and round
the double-deck red buses
hard black taxis
they ride the sound of hammers.

In Hyde Park, night loiters around the chestnut
the plane trees and sumacs are gently

pulling in curtains. It's time to disembark
from all this green, to rush the stairs and crush
some foreign fellow on the platform
at Fenchurch Street station, against a slowing train.

Four Vignettes from Devonshire

> *I'm eighty-two now. It's a badge of honour.*
> — Doris

1.
Aunt Doris parts her
regency-style striped curtains
with urns, crests of ferns
to show me the Devon hills
but when I turn from the glass, the room is full of
lace sheers, crucifixes, medieval Christs.

> *I see the hairdresser every week*
> *Jane's done it for donkey's years*
> *I can't raise my hands to set it in curlers*
> *My hair's almost all white and limp, you see.*

Her tremulous voice belies her steel spine
because I'm here, she sips her wine
to keep me, the visitor from Canada, from running off
on my own, these evenings, though I have
nowhere to go.
She's learning again to socialise
to turn the TV off, or at least to not doze off
during *The Weakest Link.*

When I'm gone she'll keep the half-bottle another week
out of curiosity perhaps, the idea of drinking by herself
too much like being sinful in this narrow flat.

She continues with the quiz shows, soaps
and snooker championships —

> Christopher is repeating
> himself. Does he think I'm deaf?
> He's always turning down the TV.

She wakes, startled.

He's still here. He's saying something about
his broken camera, about buying another
with which to take my picture.

His accent twangs like a guitar, like it was 1958
and he had just been born. Then my brother John went
away to Canada.

2.

Doris gives me a wink and a furtive smile
then rails at the television commentator for jinxing
her favourite player —

Oh Gerry, last year's champion has a particularly difficult
approach to the yellow ball.
I don't think he'll be able to sink it with this shot.
she calls this
          "Putting the mockers on him."

Daily worries soon intrude.
The new toaster tends to burn bread on one side
no matter how low the setting.

If I show Christopher's new book of poems to Father Pat
what will he think? Even Christopher has said it contains
some bad words. And will Christopher be all right in church,
does he take communion in Canada, I wonder? I dare not ask.
Will it rain tomorrow? I should have reserved a car for him to rent.
We could have driven everywhere, no matter the weather.
Is he enjoying himself?

3.

A plane tree blooms on the boulevard
and at night, the sky seems grey and

leaves of ruddy-red
hang like a thousand smudges
under street lamps,
to light the avenue of a stranger's dream.

I go to Mass, in the role of an atheist singing
his gratitude to God, with
this community of the pretty comfortable
the rarely tempted, the fully diversified.

Outside, Doris introduces me
to Father Pat and when I speak of poetry
his eyes light up; he asks Doris to bring my book next time.
I know she won't; she'll say I forgot to give her a copy.
She'll hide the books I leave behind when he visits her.
He blesses me.

4.

After the Second World War, my mother's and father's families dispersed
and uncles and aunts vanished into the remnants of Empire —
before I could meet them they had turned
to settlement, to the habits of new lands.
Birthday cards ceased and Season's Greetings came
late or not at all. Doris sent cards for years without reply.

At five to nine, back in my guest flat, loneliness shows me
the ticking clock, a spider in the window.

> Dear Janice,
> I want to accompany this postcard
> be there when you open your mailbox
> to have you find me inside. Or at least this five-star photograph
> of what Devon would look like if it was not October
> and raining every day.

Plumbing and Roofs

The only good plumbing was what
was left by the Romans.

— Mick, the roofer

When my Mick goes abroad
'e spends too much time lookin' at roofs
A-frame, flat, tile, shingle, or slate
it makes no difference
'e's a roofer by trade
Gawd lad, give it a rest, I say

'e maintains a Roman roof he saw
when we went to France five years ago —
'e calls it Gaul — was the most beautiful thing 'e'd ever seen
clay from the days of Christ

After a lifetime of doing other people's hot an' messy work
fixing their disasters an' doin' his own customers and all
you'd think 'e'd not even want to look up, it's not like
the roof is the apex of a person's life, it's just a hat
on a house really

An' you know we were down in Portsmouth last year
'e pointed out a thatched roof from Elizabeth the First's time
you'd think it was the crown jewels, Tower of London.
I had to admire the metal net they'd put on to keep the birds off it
barbed wire like, and him grinning at that whacking
great mattress keeping out the sun and rain
four hundred years on, an ancient straw bed on the top
resisting Nature and the miracles of a Monday morning
after a week 'a holidays

Lincolnshire Darkness

single lanes
narrow
farmhouses disappear below hills with
the horizon, puffs of sheep and tufts of trees
fade to dusk
as road signs and cell towers lose themselves —
a new stench is rising
shit and strength
blood of crows and badgers

night has begun to trump the day
to collapse the grid
it takes a dog with
real guts to bark aloud, beyond the shed light

the bus has left and the forest seems
to have grown
you will be taken fresh or decomposed
you might as well run
deep into the words of your prayer

the ground is not interested in your traveller's cheques
or funny foreign coins that
rust

all that is due
will be taken from you
including your whimpers on the subject of mercy —
curl fingers, deepen those cuts
in the palms of your hands

your coat was hooked away by a low
branch hours ago
on your knees you hear
something in the brush —
what would you give for
a few layers
of new-grown fur?

I love you, Scottish Widows PLC

Elderly nun in blue and white habit
overlooks the cliffs. Sees —
in cinematic black-and-white —
a battle between
Atlantic waves and English rock.

A hood and cape,
and a lovely young model with pouting red lips
combine with the Scottish Widows company
to sell retirement planning, loans and mutual funds.
Not mourning, but seducing in black
with stockings. Black being
a colour that rarely needs an adjective
is never seen as light black, off-black
muddy black, forest black, or bright black.
We're in the black.
You're in debt.
That would be the red department,
as in lingerie,
next web site over.

When your gratitude to our management
runs to the back of your throat
and tangles in your epiglottis, you'll need
the plunger of love to pull it out. Some powerful
utterance that will overwhelm your natural
shyness. When you and she are grateful, finally
when you can even acknowledge each other
after the years of taking for granted
that you and she would always be there, and together
and with money, it might well be considered
that a state of love exists
between you two and our company
and that some final words may be whispered
warmly, into your ears.

Receiving an International Phone Call from Canada

First ring. We begin to adjust our attitude
out of the torpor of BBC World Report.
I shift a hand, expect
I'll have to explain
I want to say why
OK, let it build up a bit
can't think, my mind is something
volcanic, a fountain of scalding heat from
the ocean floor, I can't let out my words in a stream
or explode like a blocked chimney.
You have the right to hear from me. You're phoning.

Not even an elaborate metaphor
can forestall the moment
I must pick up the handset
before you get fed up and hang up
no answering machine here
how melodic these new digital ring tones
blasting out Eine Kleine Nachtmusik
the first ten bars of Beethoven's Fifth Symphony
as God is my butler —
There's a call for you sir.

What can I say?
How to explain? I've been out all day. No, I was alone.
Didn't see much of anything.
No poetry. Not as such, no.
How is my uncle, how is my auntie?
Getting along alright, can't say too much
They're in the next room, small flat yes
you realise. Good. Meat and deep-fried veg twice a day.
Oh yeah, food's great, wash it down with beer. No. Not really.
The tea? Yeah, the tea is great, but it's cold.

The Rain

strokes and calms a troubled heart trying to settle
a young bird trying to learn where it can go
when all the best perches are taken.

It has been three weeks since the hijackings in America —
here in England, we see an innocent white van on the corner
and imagine
it could explode
so many of the lads now wear official
National League baseball caps
bought at The Gap, worn at Starbucks.
England — nation of hip-hop balladeers
some are in this pub tonight, playing quiz
for one of the prizes on that table:
Who won the F.A. Cup in 1956?

No. Sorry.
We've become too anxious about silver wings
about jets and fuel and soft skins that make love
to think straight. We don't even understand the rain outside
we are obsessed with airplanes flown
into skyscrapers, we're thinking of lives
lost every night, but tonight of those
who worked in offices
who cried out
and were not answered.

Dust, paper, nightmare of a snow that will not melt —
Here, the green lawns of English houses
narrow streets, gutters and drains
there is a rain in our hearts which cannot be relieved.
We are full of powder, the remnants of two towers
The bulls fled down to Battery Park
we saw them rush straight
into the Hudson river
their skins on fire.

For days the dust rose
and ash settled on the shoulders of suit jackets.
The living worked for the dead
ashen with heroism.
The crowd covered their eyes
afraid to see how the wind was trying
to cleanse the square for seven days.
At last the rain came and dissolved their disbelief —
prepared their broken bodies for the grave.

Trying to Decipher the Labels at the Uffizi Gallery

Two children run while their parents
stride through this room filled with
a Reubens, a Rembrandt, and paintings by Jan van den Hoeke.

They saw the ruins while they were in Rome
here they see paintings of the ruins of Rome
along with numerous executions
the moments before the stabbings
or after the beheadings
and of course, we see many times
the living body of St. Sebastian, arrows protruding
his face indifferent or agonized
depending on how the artist felt that day
or the look on the face of his model.

God is always stern.
Here is the Virgin Mary as a young
daydreaming babysitter.
See the middle-aged face
on the bambino Christ? There he is again —
patron of the arts redone as a duke, in armour.
The reclining nude is a seductive noble-woman
or a whore, it's hard to tell, even after I've squinted
at the label written in Italian.

The death of Adonis, naked.
The Graces look on.
The security guards are discussing a grievance.
When I reach the Botticelli room and see
the *Madonna of the Pomegranate*, with her
band of handsome teenagers in the background
I am relieved they are clothed.
In *The Annunciation*
the angel seems to have fallen into the room from the sky
Mary looks down and twists as if she would flee
and I realize
everyone
seems to have been imagining
a more perfect life to come.

At the Pantheon

Through twenty-foot doors, a dove
flies into a shaft of light
that splits the darkening morning
from the open dome above.
Rain to come, tourists are few.
Janitors sweep the marble floor
on which the flood will shortly fall.

Jesus, the apostles, and all
the bad actors of the Renaissance
ignore this.
They're examining stigmata, gazing heavenwards
as they have for hundreds of years.
If you've got a halo
you can stand on clouds and not fall
your family around you too.

Under framed Florentine-blue skies
before the marble faces of the martyrs and the popes
before the haze of history
flies the dove —
                              a black dart
across
the dismal squares of God's Portrait Artists.

Up and up
turning in a narrowing gyre
she swerves out of shadow
rides the sun-shaft
pops from the Pantheon
as from a bottle, into the open world
leaving a wingless tourist
to the dregs of antiquity.

Little Known Points of Interest
(an addenda to Frommers)

1.

Lorenzo di Lottario: a minor Florentine
during the reign of the Medici whose
primary contribution to the Renaissance
was the monetization of arts patronage
by means of selling
50-50 tickets from his wooden cart by
the dome of Santa Maria del Fiore.

2.

One euro is charged for the English-language version
of A Guide to the Cloakroom at
the Vatican Museum.

3.

The city of Rome, recognizing good patronage
has commissioned a small monument in marble —
                    to The Foreign Tourist —
to be erected next to the Bureau of Excess Luggage
where those who overpack
may find relief.

At the Metropolitan Museum of Art

The corridor opens
into an air conditioned history of Egypt
      and a stone lion
           that once watched the Nile
           from outside a pharaoh's window.
New York's human tide swells
      floods past his ears
and hooded eyes.

The security guard beside him
is waiting to retire. His jaw juts
with authority and pride
his paunch hidden by the blue jacket
three brassy buttons, grey slacks.
He is thinking of the latest edict
of the Borough of Manhattan: the new policy
      on overtime.
The lion recalls
           three dynasties of kings.

From time to time, the guard stands aside
to let a visitor photograph the lion
           poised on the only plinth
he's ever known, with weight and strength
the sculptor shaped out of stone
for his eternal vigilance.

Gravity helps everyone do their duty
the guard to hold his place
the lion to leap and kill.

           But the lion is still
and for many years has been concerned with
           the sensations of settling
           of wearing into smaller parts
worries that perhaps

the illusion is finally breaking down.

Members of the Egyptology department are
like ticks on his hide.
They fuss and cleanse.
                        His back and flanks are pitted
his eyes have weakened
                from the weight of the imperium, from scrutinizing

                        objects as useless as pink sparkling granite
                and slave-powered galleys
        in the sun.

His guard
can let out a quiet fart
                better than anyone on staff
                at the Metropolitan Museum of Art.

For the duration of this shift
neither lion or man are to be trifled with
the schoolchildren are not to touch
his long tail tucked round a hind leg
the tuft end snug on his back haunches.
His cracked, cemented snout must not be petted
            lest it cease to imply the fangs
                the deterrent.

Only the lion's feet and claws remain
of his ferocity, of his potential
            to rise and scatter these children
                screaming
at his massive stoniness

                You can see too
how New York is actually a dream
a wind that moves the sand
                against his thighs.

Our Night at the Tony Awards

Down the Avenue of the Americas
I walk tonight, looking for you

Police barricades surround
Radio City Music Hall
Light streaks from the oil-wet pavement —
the lonely crowd sings to itself, for the wait
for the stars
may be longer than the slack black limos
whose chrome tints stretch
bounce back   from the glass

Avenue of the Americas
road of hope
            where side streets end at watery docks
where a flash bulb dies in the instant
it lives
                        only   the image
of the goddess
endures beyond the
made-up lovers, and the imaginary love
in a city famous for its New Yorkness.

Within the throng
some unbelievable luck has put you close by.
I watch your gaze turn up to the
round Art deco features of these buildings
that shrug thick drips of rain
into our raised faces.
Your camera's up to catch
what I will never see till we are home —
the surfaces of city stone
the grains and lines
that extend every way
                            out
into thoughts of woods and fields

where all this began with the pioneers.

The massed right angles, the bulky height
        of this city
you seem to carry in your leather bag
photo flashes, a tripod, a sore shoulder.

But before I can cut through the shivering mob
Sara Jessica Parker, a speed-wrapped Doulton stick-figure of black silk
affecting a royal walk not at all —
skates across behind the middle-aged cop (a suburban house in Jersey)
                the cop you will tell me you were just getting to know —
and whumpf, she jumps into a limo.

They scream,
        for another long black gleam
                                of car   has jerked ahead
while Sara's paramour
Matthew The Broderick
        appears next
in the gap between the famous and the handlers.
                        He's giving roses to the ladies! He's coming our way!

        Suddenly, he thrusts his last two roses at you
blows a kiss   turns at the shrill
Matt!!
Limo door open, irritated blonde glaring
        he trots, falls into the car.

You blush over his yellow roses
their muslin aroma
        more screams, you turn
a large camera lens rolls in the gutter
the policeman and I both bend and grasp
his warm hand over mine.

My wife, it's hers, I say.
Drop it.

He rises, glares at me, and with
his large cop-authority, standard-issue hand gently
passes you the lens. You accept.
The roses bob madly.

We saunter back to the hotel
your hands wide, a rose in each
I lug your bag of lenses, film, tripod, et cetera

In the elevator mirrors, you grin, elated.
At last, in our room
you fall, strangely wild
onto the bed, on which I laid
less than an hour ago and watched the Tonys
on TV, while you waited
outside Radio City Music Hall
in the rain.

Union Station

A chain surrounds the city
while we, the citizens ride
our machine, grease splattering our hands and faces.

After the working day, and out of breath
we race to the basement of
Union Station, where rails and trains unite.

One floor above, my eyes rise
up cool sandy columns that hold the canopy
of this great hall, a patterned sky

and as if on a beach, I relax
and evaporate, rise out of my self
and walk in space, a child astronaut

on the end of a balloon. I'm up near
limestone walls to better see
those Roman letters stride suggestively

and evoke the antiquity of Prince Rupert
the ancient fortress of Hamilton
the jungle gardens of Saskatoon!
        (and to ungratefully wish for cities
                named Peace, Love, and Imagine That).

Worn steps lead down
and down into modernity, into millions of voices,
trapped in a rising river on the lower floor —

Up here, in spaciousness
someone speaks seductively into a phone —
I descend, vesper-quiet, eavesdrop.

Then, as if it was a tip, I spy a dime
shining on the floor at end of day —
someone's loss, and it might be mine
a sliver of the thing I had to say.

My suitcase

has taken buses, trains, and planes
has shown my lumpen packing
and underwear to security —
at Paddington Station my slow crab-like drag
broke one of its wheels
so I performed the dead-weight jerk
as if hefting someone up stairs, over tracks
down long platforms —
real things being never so real as when
you must carry them through changed plans
misunderstood instructions
past the rolled eyes
of foreigners in their own streets
watching a stranger lost and
in a hurry.

My suitcase patiently revealed
something from home every day —
an excess of this, an overweight of that.
I've worn out the line
about not buying Greek busts at the British Museum
but must confess to carting home marbles
that reminded me of
the moon and planets
glistening in my hand.

At home, I separate the few clean
from the many dirty
empty my intimacy onto the bed
shunt my suitcase into the basement.

Trips end as they begin
with coins and stamps unspent
foreign kings, queens, inventors now imported
heroes of wars I can't remember
to be fixed to postcards I forgot to send.

Alternative Destinations

Poem for a Dream Bookstore

From the dark foyer
I see aisles, shelves, covers
set aglow by a neon moon
that casts a cold breath
on my naked shoulder
limp pyjamas in a puddle.

Fingers drift down spine after spine
as if they can read the ink
compensate for the dark.

               I want the book not written
the one not for sale, its words etched in the ribs
packed in the liver, unread, unvoiced.
Let's print no more shambles
through our dappled youth
waste no more time recounting
how we've wasted time
unless we want those last few readers
to slam the book down, go to the movies
hit the road, guitars in their cases, amps in the van.

I find myself on the shelf
a stock card between other names.
The staff are asleep
in their beds like the best kinds
of minor characters, adding
texture to the wind
rushing up my bare back.
I'm afraid this time I'm actually really
standing naked in a dream bookstore after all
while outside, the clouds let down drizzle
into creaking, cold gutters.

Jiu-Jitsu with Death

A collector works through his numbers to relax:
       the second George V penny
       a six-cent stamp on a first day cover
       the third issue of Superman's Girlfriend Lois Lane.
Worth fluctuates.
Any complete and perfect set is over and
dead. Ready to be sold.
Avoid such certainty, with gentle skill.

An eye skims a shelf and
stops at every gap —
the dream that disappears
a minute after waking
Tip of tongue, *I just had it*
          a fragment like
cool marbles that roll and click
            at play.

Sometimes an object from childhood
will deflect your opponent's weight
apply jiu-jitsu against fear — age and time —
faithful monsters who can
exert pressure without grasp.

I swallow and swivel away —
there's Hope, and hey, look out the window
at that child. His feathered eyes
can pick out streets where
I once rode my bike, delivered newspapers
to home-owners who have moved away
leaving me to own the past.

My present self walks along shop windows
sees a young man who can sprint this busy street
and collide with no one, all the while
admiring himself, glancing

again and again at his sleek power
infinite, muscular, until   smack
into

       the glass door of realization.

Late

When I am late to the office
I slink along the wall
past policy pronouncements
printed from email
posted to partitions.
I rub against fabric, cubicles,
the inner walls of the company —
producing static electricity
shutting down computers
I pass.

Like a cartoon dog in trouble with his master
            making things worse for himself —
            until
            at my desk
I remember
                    my boss is on vacation!

Out of my soft jacket, into my computer screen
I surf to a travel site.
See? That's my boss!
See the sun, the waves, his chaise longue?
He is releasing my worked hours
like balloons, tipping the waiter on the beach
at St. Tropez with my timesheets.

When I am old my lateness
will be a credit against death
I'll let it out slow, an emission from my dark bed
as our city's factories release their sulphur
nakedly.

            I think this is a night poem about the day
                I procrastinate and droop
                        asleep
                    at pencil point

but words keep running down the page
        like shower water
filling the bed.
        Where's the faucet?
Someone send for the logical man
to carefully
stop me
here.

temp pome

This is a temp rarity of a pome.
It is instructional entertaining
for ~~hominid~~ hominoid units.

Soon we issue version 2.0
of this pome. New version will be compatible
with all thinking since installation
of university degree 1.0, 1.1, or 1.2.1
or high school diploma 5.5 or higher.
This pome will be compatible with all other
texts and pomes written last year
running on the comprehensive
Anguish Text System (ATS).

The rapid depreciation of this pome
does not indicate is obsolete at time of publication.
The manufacturer depletes a rapidly expanding
inventory of pomes
and slackening demand, leading to price deflation in
the market for pomes.

The distributor warrants this pome to be free of defects
for a period of ninety (90) days and keeping with the
licensing agreement.

Because, this temp rarity of pome may not be presented
as part of a symposia, conference, or a lecture seriousness, without
prior permission of the license-holder. In the event of expiry while
in use, the writer of the pome, hereafter described as the content
provider, assumes no liability, impleyed or expressively rendered.

Nineteen Corruptions of Tai Chi

Slap paint on house.
Conceal facts to avoid argument.
Wave at departing train.

A sleepy child surfs the web.
Cancel fitness club membership.
Buy high, sell low.
New car rusts slowly.

Consult day timer at night.
Lovers need money.
Watch riot after pro sports championship.
Eat TV-dinner beside old radio.

Butterfly plays the trombone.
Remove headphones at trickling brook.
Modify body with paper cuts.
Endure an obnoxious waitress.

Leave umbrella on the bus.
Erase two lines of a poem.
Smile at your photo identification.
Forget dental appointment.

New Readings of Shakespeare

Such eagerness
joy with finish and be praised
for reading passage loud
from
Macbeth
in halting
English

My high school students from China
are nervous and proud
of having come to Canada and spent their
parents' new wealth in such an odd pursuit
what Mother expects, none can say

Meanwhile Duncan is slain and his guards
have been slaughtered to take the blame
before they can protest their innocence. This morning
we read a story together in the Globe
about foreigners in their fifth year in Canadian jails
without due process
subject to speechlessness and threat of rendition
because politicians fear defeat in the next election —
real men turned into story characters
improper rendering: *mojibake*.

> If a suicide bomber chickens out in the middle
> of the business district, does he make a sound?

Student omits definite article
creates ideograms above
words, in the margins,
makes Shakespeare Chinese —
the play will lose much
in Mandarin, but perhaps more
will be gained by this young girl who brings
meaning into focus

misery into light
where it might be helped
by sunshine this morning

Back Home

inserts itself into the halting talk
of foreign students longing to belong
longing to be
                    back home
and the school uniform does not hide
slumped shoulders
like the impression of a body in rumpled bedclothes
does not hide

from Hong Kong to Gambia these boys
speak of where-ness and here-ness
but English is still such an obstacle race
of metaphors like obstacle race
their minds full of letters, symbols
theorems of calculus
and all the rules

where newspapers write one way
and the principal scolds in another
and the people on TV don't speak in complete sentences
and the teachers are
in such a rush
they overlook
or cannot remember how to explain what makes a sentence
                    run on
and the rules for commas or why Shakespeare's kings
            and noblemen
are not noble or men like criminal *Lady Mack-Beff*

every English writer with a million choices
and the foreign student tries
to understand one, to not stumble
or turn her back on her parents' desire
that she become a business executive
though one or two students have run away into the Canadian enormity —

so much space
        no crowded

then she says   *I like art and music*
and fashion and hanging about in such a clean city —
        like Hamilton
innocence abroad and speaking true

Underwater

for Bill Everett, creator of the Sub-Mariner

Into the streams and seaweed
we sent our eyes
into the fold in the paper
and came upon
a merman full of rage
and his blue-skinned race
withering in the canyons
of the Atlantic ocean.

The merman immediately accused us
— kids with paper routes —
of polluting and destroying
the underwater currents that sustained them
of eradicating his tribe
with our poor waste disposal practices
and relentless weapons testing
Eventually, as an air-breather and surface-dweller
I came to know *guilt* and *environment.*

And I was pleased
a fictional character had noticed me.
He was tragic and full of self-pity.
He took oxygen from water with the
gills in his neck.
I understood racial difference
What do you breathe?

His mother blue, father white
he had fallen from her womb
into a warm geyser
the bubbles hissed across his eyes
he woke —
to see her smiling face.

That loving flashback
left me breathless in the sun-setting park
and now, too late —
a box of comics bounced in the bike carrier
as I flew down rutted roads
home to my scolding mother
and me always late for dinner.

Like Narcissus

I fell into a pond and drowned
became mute and bloated.
My lips were cleansed, my hair became
entwined among the water lilies.

In this green and darker place
I am sustained by the belief every soul is a gem made by God
to one day be raised up
by others to a greater state.

There will be no pedestal; I imagine
someone is hammering
a coffin together from a kit they bought at
the hardware superstore.

Either my vain past or
my belief in resurrection is false —
yet at its surface, the water above me seems to be evaporating
in the noonday sun.

The moon over clouds

is high and bright
at midnight
the plane's wings glint
and drive home the harder truth
about eye light —

I'm a reflection of myself
even without glass or mirror
we are servants of a sun
that bounces moonlight into mind
so it can be reflected back
out
onto this page

Under Old Stars (Norris Point, Nfld.)

sky blue to royal blue to black
and remember why we're here —
to slow and forget
to hear an invitation drawled by the town: *See? Sea.*
and the water laughs

First Venus,
then Mars appears behind
those skids of clouds evaporating
left and right —
        moose are reverting into trees
        milky star-light sings
sotto voce
some nights cannot be pierced
or eaten away by a series of wriggling facts
from astronomy books or mythology

        let's cast a line into
a place so empty
        it pulls, and notice how much
           it hurts
           that the gods ascended into the night and left us
helpless
almost falling off the harbour dock

after an hour, the night's black drape
           begins to thin. Some points of light
are leaking
through this theatrical fabric
Orion connect-the-dots, and
hard-working Hesiod weaves a story
so that threads will yield one by one, and give back a little
of what is past, and what's to come

to fade away without the shock of death
to remember where we came from
before anyone wakes
across the water

Trespassing

is a singularly good-looking word
but ashamed, appearing in public so often
in black and glossy letters
on white enamel signs

shining so brightly
in the cold and furtive night
it must have sinned a great sin
long ago

for it always travels with **No**
the ball that's
chained to the convict's ankle
chafing and burning the skin

Poetry for Restaurants

is like guitarists who make recordings
of how late they came to the perfection
of their licks, having doodled away their youth
in the corner of a restaurant
while rich women chattered over wine sauces
and navy blue napkins

poetry for restaurants
is like the waiters who have over-acted in Stratford
all the while auditioning for other dining establishments
so they can afford better living quarters
closer to the stage, the better to observe
the younger and younger competition
and to stew in their own simmering potential

and what is it about food and art?
that a series of photographs, acrylics or oils should
hang above, gathering the soot
of stuttering candles
should hang over the heads of those who just want to get
this romance over with?
Or to get into her panties
or perhaps it's Father's Day
and now we talk over folded hands, with one eye on
the Stanley Cup finals over the bar.

I'm probably reading this poem to you in a bar
and I'm wondering how many drinks you've had
and what the next line should be
and whether I should have stopped
one line before this.

41 South Street at Night

in the parking lot of the nursing home
        cars that have rumbled
all day long   find rest

their drivers however
        keep idling over the state
of a mother's finances
        the sight of a father's hand punctured
        for intravenous therapy
they are getting to know the smell of earth
and although they see Jesus with his arms raised
in every room
        they can only stomach for so long
their fear
        the cherry darkness of blood

by the front door
        a raccoon
                leaps out of the bin
                    with a bun in its mouth
they sigh, giggle
        someone lights a cigarette
another is cadged
        with a smile
and suddenly
        they hear the choir
that's been singing tonight —
thousands of frogs in the ravines
        pushing up pillars of sound

one of them wanders off among the green dwarf pines
        to cry for a parent
who does not recognize him any more

he wants to join the chorus
        to sing his own lyric

about tides and the moon,
        lose himself in these tangible woods
like an uncertain ember
        life-span
four minutes or less

Before the Sun Rises

In the hour before sunrise
dark turns to a bluish bruise
even the insomniacs are asleep
since few may see every hour in the twenty-four
nor hear the wind move in the hall
and bedroom, choosing us one by one.

At midnight
or when the moon is rising above a field
a heart does not stop by accident
except in the minds of mourners.
Someone had the timing
to get it done tonight
before the birds woke
and throats began to clear.

Those with broken limbs
condemned to healing
doze under a throbbing ache.
They ask their sweaty pillow
if they are being punished
and then —
confounded by
the cold, obscure sun —
forgetfulness sets in.

Notes on the Poems

In "At Wanuskewin, Saskatchewan," *wanuskewin* is a Cree word meaning, seeking peace of mind or living in harmony.

In "I love you Scottish Widows PLC," Scottish Widows refers to a British financial organization that sells insurance, banking and investment products. Presently, it is part of the Lloyds Banking Group.

In "Trying to Decipher the Labels at the Uffizi Gallery," the observation that the angel in Boticelli's *The Cestello Annunciation* (c. 1489) seems to fall into the room comes from *The Uffizi Gallery* (Guinti Editore S.p.A., Florence, 2001) p. 136.

In "New Readings of Shakespeare," *mojibake* is a loanword from Japanese meaning, improper rendering of characters by a computer operating system.

Acknowledgements

For their good advice and unflagging encouragement I am grateful to
Richard Harrison, Noelle Allen, Maria Jacobs, Donna Langevin, Sue
Chenette, Lindsay Hodder, Allan Briesmaster, Paul Sutherland, and
Russell Thornton. Additionally, members of *the new writing workshop*
and the Lit Live Reading Series offered valuable help during the writing
of these poems.

Thanks to the editors of the following magazines where some of these
poems first appeared: *Carousel, The Antigonish Review, Hammered
Out, Kairos, Dream Catcher (U.K.), Contemporary Verse 2, Grain,* and
Dusty Owl.

"41 South Street at Night" was a finalist in ARC's 2007 Poem of the
Year contest and "The Way She Loves Him" — received the 2007
Hamilton Public Library Award for Best Individual Poem.

Thank you Janice Jackson, for the cover photograph and your
perpetual support of my writing. Kudos to Leigh Kotsilidis for the cover
design and layouts.

Finally, this book is for the men and women of Hamilton's Disabled and
Aged Regional Transit System (DARTS) — those who ride and those
who drive the buses, and those who work behind the scenes to make
the whole shebang function on a daily basis. You have inspired more
than a few of these poems.

Chris Pannell is part of the organizing committee for the Hamilton reading series Lit Live and also serves on the board of Hamilton's annual gritLIT Literary Festival. He has published two poetry books: *Under Old Stars* (2002) and *Sorry I Spent Your Poem* (1999). He is also the author of a set of three poetry broadsheets entitled, *Fractures, Subluxations and Dislocations* which won the Hamilton & Region Arts Council poetry book award in 1997. From 1993 until 2005 he ran the New Writing Workshop at Hamilton Artists Inc. and edited two book-length anthologies for the group. He has been published in literary magazines across Canada and internationally as well. *Drive* is his fourth collection of poetry.